THIS BOOK IS THE PROPERTY OF:

			Book No. ______
STATE	________________		Enter information
PROVINCE	________________		in spaces
COUNTY	________________		to the left as
PARISH	________________		instructed
SCHOOL DISTRICT	________________		
OTHER	________________		

ISSUED TO	Year Used	CONDITION	
		ISSUED	RETURNED
- - - - - - - -	- - - -	- - - -	- - - -
- - - - - - - -	- - - -	- - - -	- - - -

PUPILS to whom this textbook is issued must not write on any page or mark any part of it in any way, consumable textbooks excepted.

1. Teachers should see that the pupil's name is clearly written in ink in the spaces above in every book issued.
2. The following terms should be used in recording the condition of the book: New; Good; Fair; Poor; Bad.

TO THE STUDENT

These *Recycling Problem Working Papers* are to be used in the study of Chapters 1–24 of CENTURY 21 ACCOUNTING.

Blank forms are provided for each Recycling Problem. Printed on each page is the number of the problem in the textbook for which the form is to be used. Also shown is a specific instruction number for which the form is to be used. The Recycling Problems are in Appendix E of the textbook.

You may not be required to use every form that is provided. Your teacher will tell you whether to retain or dispose of the unused pages.

The pages are perforated so they may be removed as the work required in each assignment is completed. The pages will be more easily detached if you crease the sheet along the line of perforations and then remove the sheet by pulling sideways rather than upward.

Contents

1   Starting a Proprietorship: Changes that Affect the Accounting Equation   1

2   Analyzing Transactions into Debit and Credit Parts   3

3   Journalizing Transactions   5

4   Posting to a General Ledger   7

5   Cash Control Systems   11

6   Work Sheet for a Service Business   13

7   Financial Statements for a Proprietorship   15

8   Recording Adjusting and Closing Entries for a Service Business   17

9   Journalizing Purchases and Cash Payments   19

10   Journalizing Sales and Cash Receipts Using Special Journals   23

11   Posting to General and Subsidiary Ledgers   27

12   Preparing Payroll Records   37

13   Payroll Accounting, Taxes, and Reports   39

14   Distributing Dividends and Preparing a Work Sheet for a Merchandising Business   41

15   Financial Statements for a Corporation   45

16   Recording Adjusting and Closing Entries for a Corporation   51

17   Accounting for Uncollectible Accounts Receivable   63

18   Accounting for Plant Assets and Depreciation   67

19   Accounting for Inventory   71

20   Accounting for Notes and Interest   73

21   Accounting for Accrued Revenue and Expenses   77

22   End-of-Fiscal-Period Work for a Corporation   82

23   Accounting for Partnerships   91

24   Recording International and Internet Sales   97

Extra Forms   99

1-1 RECYCLING PROBLEM, p. E-1

Determining how transactions change an accounting equation

Trans. No.	Assets				= Liabilities	+ Owner's Equity
	Cash	+ Accts. Rec.—Dean Mills	+ Supplies	+ Prepaid Insurance	= Accts. Pay.—Topline	+ Brian Frizza, Capital
Beg. Bal. 1.	2,200 −120	− 0 −	1,100	200	200	3,300 −120 (expense)
New Bal. 2.	2,080	− 0 −	1,100	200	200	3,180
New Bal. 3.						
New Bal. 4.						
New Bal. 5.						
New Bal. 6.						
New Bal. 7.						
New Bal. 8.						
New Bal. 9.						
New Bal. 10.						
New Bal. 11.						
New Bal. 12.						
New Bal. 13.						
New Bal. 14.						
New Bal. 15.						
New Bal.						

2-1 RECYCLING PROBLEM, p. E-2

Analyzing transactions into debit and credit parts

3-1 RECYCLING PROBLEM, p. E-3

Journalizing transactions and proving and ruling a journal

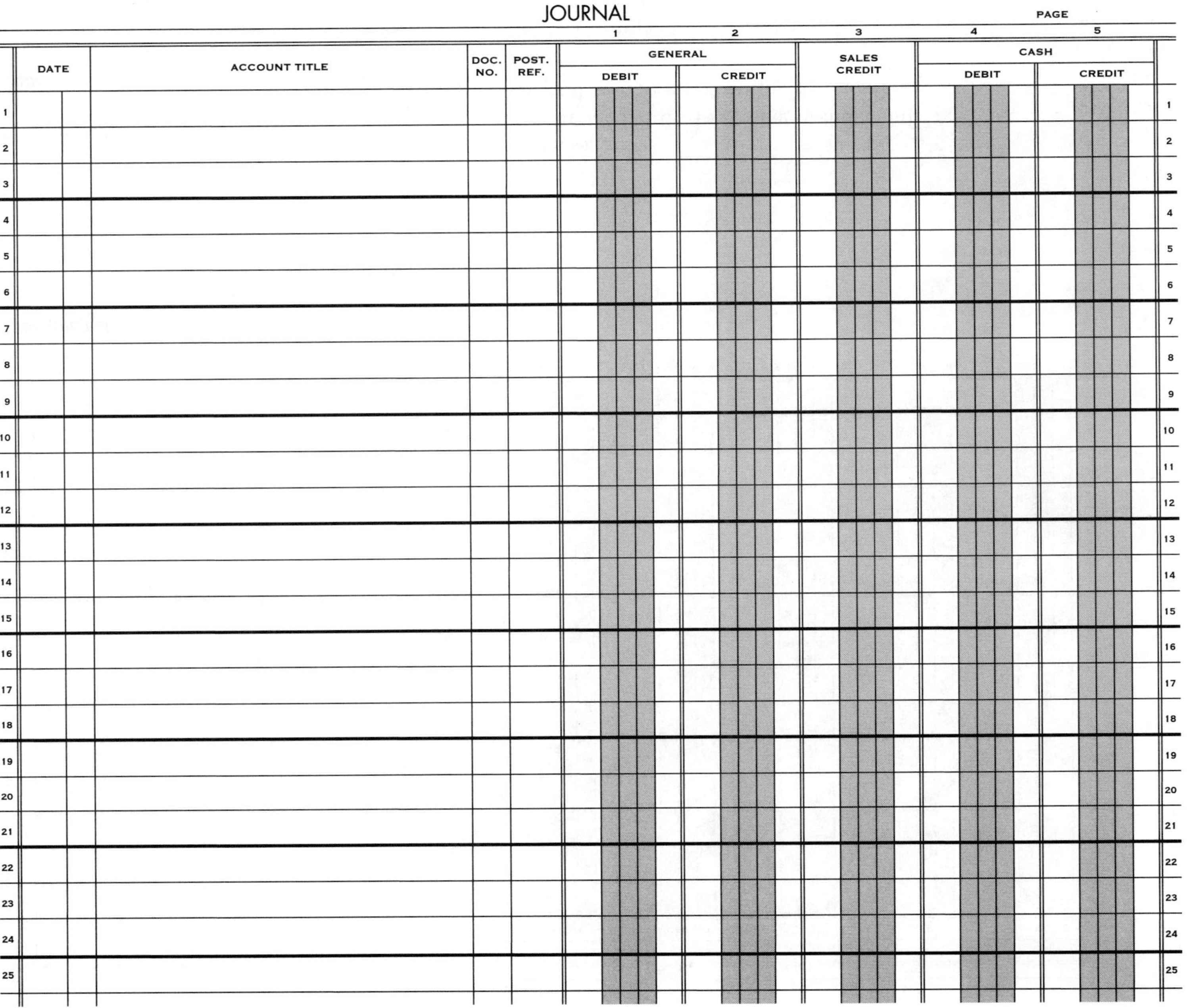

JOURNAL

PAGE 5

DATE	ACCOUNT TITLE	DOC. NO.	POST. REF.	1 GENERAL DEBIT	2 GENERAL CREDIT	3 SALES CREDIT	4 CASH DEBIT	5 CASH CREDIT

Prove page 1 of the journal:

Column	Debit Column Totals	Credit Column Totals
General		
Sales		
Cash		
Totals		

Prove page 2 of the journal:

Column	Debit Column Totals	Credit Column Totals
General		
Sales		
Cash		
Totals		

Prove cash:

Cash on hand at the beginning of the month ....

Plus total cash received during the month ....

Equals Total ....

Less total cash paid during the month ....

Equals cash balance at the end of the month ....

Checkbook balance on the next unused check stub ....

4-1 RECYCLING PROBLEM, p. E-4

Journalizing transactions and posting to a general ledger

2., 5., 6.

JOURNAL

PAGE 1

					1	2	3	4	5
					GENERAL		SALES CREDIT	CASH	
DATE	ACCOUNT TITLE	DOC. NO.	POST. REF.		DEBIT	CREDIT		DEBIT	CREDIT

3. *Prove the journal:*

Column	Debit Column Totals	Credit Column Totals
General	________	________
Sales	________	________
Cash	________	________
Totals	========	========

4. *Prove cash:*

Cash on hand at the beginning of the month . . . . ________

Plus total cash received during the month . . . . ________

Equals Total . . . . ________

Less total cash paid during the month . . . . ________

Equals cash balance at the end of the month . . . . ________

Checkbook balance on the next unused check stub . . . . ________

1., 6.   **GENERAL LEDGER**

ACCOUNT Cash   ACCOUNT NO. 110

DATE	ITEM	POST. REF.	DEBIT	CREDIT	BALANCE	
					DEBIT	CREDIT

ACCOUNT Accounts Receivable—Nicholas Calendo   ACCOUNT NO. 120

DATE	ITEM	POST. REF.	DEBIT	CREDIT	BALANCE	
					DEBIT	CREDIT

ACCOUNT Supplies   ACCOUNT NO. 130

DATE	ITEM	POST. REF.	DEBIT	CREDIT	BALANCE	
					DEBIT	CREDIT

ACCOUNT Accounts Payable—Jordan Supplies   ACCOUNT NO. 210

DATE	ITEM	POST. REF.	DEBIT	CREDIT	BALANCE	
					DEBIT	CREDIT

ACCOUNT Janet Porter, Capital   ACCOUNT NO. 310

DATE	ITEM	POST. REF.	DEBIT	CREDIT	BALANCE	
					DEBIT	CREDIT

4-1 RECYCLING PROBLEM (concluded)

1., 6.   **GENERAL LEDGER**

ACCOUNT Janet Porter, Drawing   ACCOUNT NO. 320

DATE	ITEM	POST. REF.	DEBIT	CREDIT	BALANCE	
					DEBIT	CREDIT

ACCOUNT Sales   ACCOUNT NO. 410

DATE	ITEM	POST. REF.	DEBIT	CREDIT	BALANCE	
					DEBIT	CREDIT

ACCOUNT Advertising Expense   ACCOUNT NO. 510

DATE	ITEM	POST. REF.	DEBIT	CREDIT	BALANCE	
					DEBIT	CREDIT

ACCOUNT Miscellaneous Expense   ACCOUNT NO. 520

DATE	ITEM	POST. REF.	DEBIT	CREDIT	BALANCE	
					DEBIT	CREDIT

ACCOUNT Rent Expense   ACCOUNT NO. 530

DATE	ITEM	POST. REF.	DEBIT	CREDIT	BALANCE	
					DEBIT	CREDIT

ACCOUNT   ACCOUNT NO.

DATE	ITEM	POST. REF.	DEBIT	CREDIT	BALANCE	
					DEBIT	CREDIT

5-1 RECYCLING PROBLEM, p. E-4

Reconciling a bank statement; journalizing a bank service charge, a dishonored check, and petty cash transactions

1., 3.

JOURNAL PAGE ___________

	DATE	ACCOUNT TITLE	DOC. NO.	POST. REF.	GENERAL DEBIT	GENERAL CREDIT	SALES CREDIT	CASH DEBIT	CASH CREDIT	
1										1
2										2
3										3
4										4
5										5
6										6
7										7
8										8
9										9
10										10
11										11
12										12

2.

RECONCILIATION OF BANK STATEMENT

_______________ (Date)

Balance On Check Stub No. ____ .... $ _______

DEDUCT BANK CHARGES:

Description	Amount
	$

Total bank charges ▶

Adjusted Check Stub Balance .... $ _______

Balance On Bank Statement .... $ _______

ADD OUTSTANDING DEPOSITS:

Date	Amount
	$

Total outstanding deposits ▶

SUBTOTAL .... $ _______

DEDUCT OUTSTANDING CHECKS:

Ck. No.	Amount	Ck. No.	Amount

Total outstanding checks ▶

Adjusted Bank Balance .... $ _______

6-1 RECYCLING PROBLEM, p. E-5

Completing a work sheet

1., 2., 3., 4., 5., 6.

ACCOUNT TITLE	TRIAL BALANCE		ADJUSTMENTS		INCOME STATEMENT		BALANCE SHEET	
	DEBIT 1	CREDIT 2	DEBIT 3	CREDIT 4	DEBIT 5	CREDIT 6	DEBIT 7	CREDIT 8

7-1 RECYCLING PROBLEM, p. E-6

Preparing financial statements

1., 2.

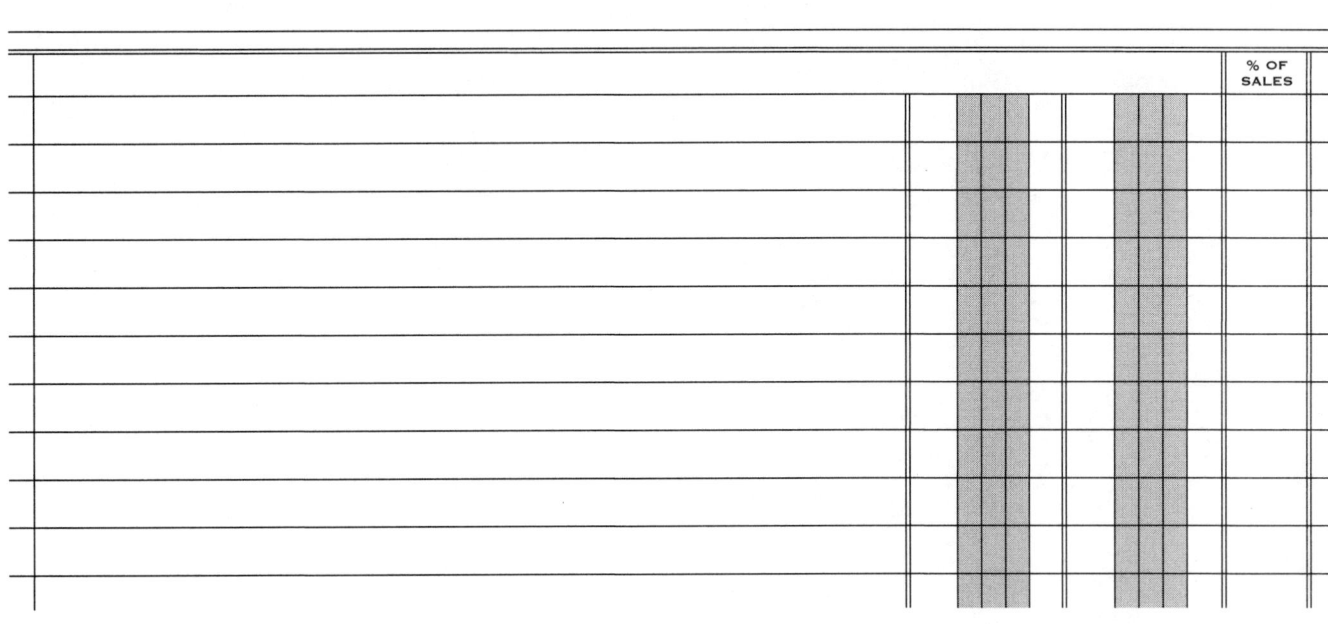

3.

8-1 RECYCLING PROBLEM, p. E-7

Journalizing adjusting and closing entries

1., 2.

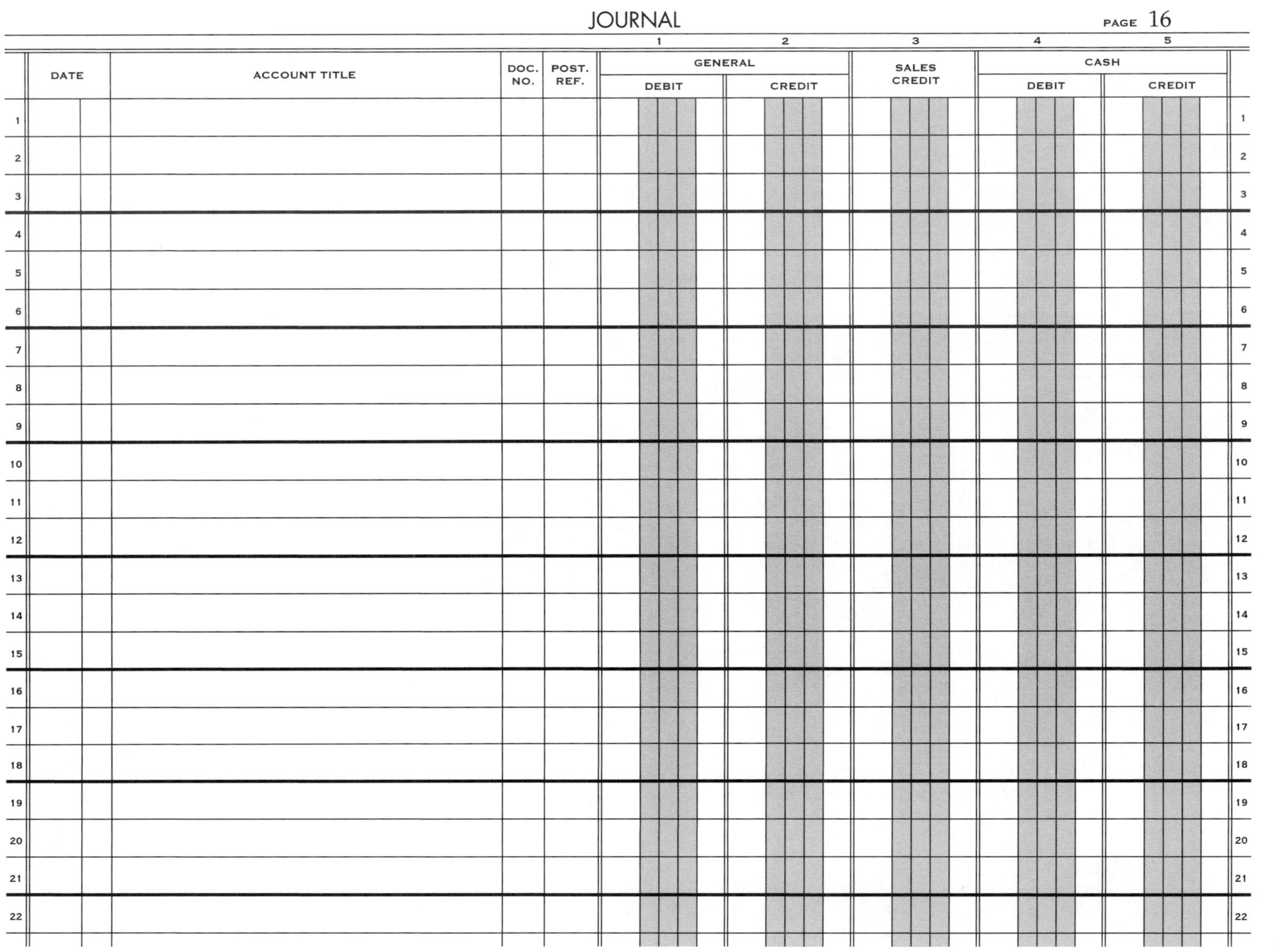

9-1 RECYCLING PROBLEM, p. E-7

Journalizing purchases, cash payments, and other transactions

1., 5.

PURCHASES JOURNAL   PAGE 9

	DATE		ACCOUNT CREDITED	PURCH. NO.	POST. REF.	PURCHASES DR. ACCTS. PAY. CR.	
1							1
2							2
3							3
4							4
5							5
6							6
7							7
8							8
9							9
10							10
11							11
12							12

CASH PAYMENTS JOURNAL

PAGE 15

DATE	ACCOUNT TITLE	CK. NO.	POST. REF.	GENERAL DEBIT	GENERAL CREDIT	ACCOUNTS PAYABLE DEBIT	PURCHASES DISCOUNT CREDIT	CASH CREDIT
				1	2	3	4	5

1., 2.

2.

Column Title	Debit Column Totals	Credit Column Totals
General Debit		
General Credit		
Accounts Payable Debit		
Purchases Discount Credit		
Cash Credit		
Totals		

9-1 RECYCLING PROBLEM (continued)

3., 4., 6., 7.

CASH PAYMENTS JOURNAL

PAGE 16

DATE	ACCOUNT TITLE	CK. NO.	POST. REF.	GENERAL DEBIT	GENERAL CREDIT	ACCOUNTS PAYABLE DEBIT	PURCHASES DISCOUNT CREDIT	CASH CREDIT
			1		2	3	4	5
1								
2								
3								
4								
5								
6								
7								
8								

6.

Column Title	Debit Column Totals	Credit Column Totals
General Debit	_______	
General Credit		_______
Accounts Payable Debit	_______	
Purchases Discount Credit		_______
Cash Credit		_______
Totals	_______	_______

1.

GENERAL JOURNAL

PAGE 12

	DATE	ACCOUNT TITLE	DOC. NO.	POST. REF.	DEBIT	CREDIT	
1							1
2							2
3							3
4							4
5							5
6							6
7							7
8							8
9							9
10							10
11							11
12							12
13							13
14							14
15							15

10-1 RECYCLING PROBLEM, p. E-8

Journalizing sales and cash receipts transactions; proving and ruling journals

1.

GENERAL JOURNAL

PAGE 17

	DATE	ACCOUNT TITLE	DOC. NO.	POST. REF.	DEBIT	CREDIT	
1							1
2							2
3							3
4							4
5							5
6							6
7							7
8							8
9							9
10							10
11							11
12							12
13							13
14							14
15							15
16							16
17							17
18							18
19							19
20							20
21							21
22							22
23							23
24							24
25							25

1., 2., 3.

SALES JOURNAL   PAGE 22

	DATE	ACCOUNT DEBITED	SALE NO.	POST. REF.	ACCOUNTS RECEIVABLE DEBIT (1)	SALES CREDIT (2)	SALES TAX PAYABLE CREDIT (3)	
1	20-- Nov. 24	Brought Forward		✔	15 9 9 6 55	15 1 4 8 25	8 4 8 30	1
2								2
3								3
4								4
5								5
6								6
7								7
8								8
9								9
10								10
11								11
12								12
13								13
14								14
15								15
16								16
17								17
18								18

2.

Col. No.	Column Title	Debit Totals	Credit Totals
1	Accounts Receivable Debit	__________	
2	Sales Credit		__________
3	Sales Tax Payable Credit		__________
	Totals	__________	__________

10-1   RECYCLING PROBLEM (concluded)

1., 4., 6.

CASH RECEIPTS JOURNAL

PAGE 23

	DATE	ACCOUNT TITLE	DOC. NO.	POST. REF.	GENERAL DEBIT	GENERAL CREDIT	ACCOUNTS RECEIVABLE CREDIT	SALES CREDIT	SALES TAX PAYABLE CREDIT	SALES DISCOUNT DEBIT	CASH DEBIT	
1	Nov. 24	Brought Forward		✓			13484 25	25118 77	1507 13	25 25	40084 90	1
2												2
3												3
4												4
5												5
6												6
7												7
8												8
9												9
10												10
11												11
12												12
13												13
14												14

4.

Col. No.	Column Title	Debit Totals	Credit Totals
1	General Debit	_________	
2	General Credit		_________
3	Accounts Receivable Credit		_________
4	Sales Credit		_________
5	Sales Tax Payable Credit		_________
6	Sales Discount Debit	_________	
7	Cash Debit	_________	
	Totals	_________	_________

5.

CASH PROOF

Cash on hand at the beginning of the month ....
Plus total cash received during the month ....
Equals total ....
Less total cash paid during the month ....
Equals cash balance on hand at end of the month ....
Checkbook balance on the next unused check stub ....

11-1   RECYCLING PROBLEM, p. E-9

Posting to general and subsidiary ledgers

1., 2.

SALES JOURNAL   PAGE 9

	DATE		ACCOUNT DEBITED	SALE NO.	POST. REF.	ACCOUNTS RECEIVABLE DEBIT	SALES CREDIT	SALES TAX PAYABLE CREDIT	
1	20-- Aug.	14	Joe Chapin	50		3 8 2 20	3 6 4 00	1 8 20	1
2		15	Susan King	51		1 8 3 75	1 7 5 00	8 75	2
3		24	Gary Voyles	52		1 9 8 45	1 8 9 00	9 45	3
4		25	Joan Aberg	53		1 3 9 65	1 3 3 00	6 65	4
5									5
6									6

1., 3.

PURCHASES JOURNAL   PAGE 9

	DATE		ACCOUNT CREDITED	PURCH. NO.	POST. REF.	PURCHASES DR. ACCTS. PAY. CR.	
1	20-- Aug.	2	Diamond T. Boots	63		2 3 1 0 00	1
2		18	Boot Town	64		1 3 1 6 00	2
3		31	Western Leather Co.	65		1 2 0 4 00	3
4							4
5							5
6							6

1.

GENERAL JOURNAL

PAGE 9

	DATE		ACCOUNT TITLE	DOC. NO.	POST. REF.	DEBIT	CREDIT	
1	Aug.	9	Supplies—Office	M30		1 8 9 00		1
2			Accounts Payable/National Supply		/		1 8 9 00	2
3		25	Sales Returns and Allowances	CM11		1 0 0 00		3
4			Sales Tax Payable			5 00		4
5			Accounts Receivable/Joe Chapin		/		1 0 5 00	5
6		27	Accounts Payable/Diamond T. Boots	DM5	/	4 2 1 00		6
7			Purchases Returns and Allow.				4 2 1 00	7
8								8
9								9

11-1 RECYCLING PROBLEM (continued)

1., 4.

CASH RECEIPTS JOURNAL   PAGE 9

	DATE	ACCOUNT TITLE	DOC. NO.	POST. REF.	GENERAL DEBIT	GENERAL CREDIT	ACCOUNTS RECEIVABLE CREDIT	SALES CREDIT	SALES TAX PAYABLE CREDIT	SALES DISCOUNT DEBIT	CASH DEBIT	
1	20-- Aug. 4	Gary Voyles	R29				367 50				367 50	1
2	5	✔	TS28					4690 00	234 50		4924 50	2
3	12	✔	TS29					5796 00	289 80		6085 80	3
4	19	✔	TS30					5712 00	285 60		5997 60	4
5	26	✔	TS31					6342 00	317 10		6659 10	5
6	28	Joan Aberg	R30				249 90				249 90	6
7	31	✔	TS32					3668 00	183 40		3851 40	7
8												8
9												9
10												10
11												11
12												12
13												13
14												14

RECYCLING PROBLEM (continued)

1., 5.

CASH PAYMENTS JOURNAL

PAGE 9

	DATE		ACCOUNT TITLE	CK. NO.	POST. REF.	GENERAL DEBIT	GENERAL CREDIT	ACCOUNTS PAYABLE DEBIT	PURCHASES DISCOUNT CREDIT	CASH CREDIT	
1	20-- Aug.	1	Rent Expense	782		1300 00				1300 00	1
2		7	Utilities Expense	783		221 34				221 34	2
3		10	Western Leather Co.	784				3276 00		3276 00	3
4		15	Yeatman Corporation	785				3500 00	70 00	3430 00	4
5		28	Boot Town	786				2072 00		2072 00	5
6		31	Supplies—Office	787		58 80				282 10	6
7			Supplies—Store	788		80 50					7
8			Advertising Expense	789		89 60					8
9			Miscellaneous Expense	786		53 15					9
10			Cash Short and Over	791		0 05					10
11											11
12											12
13											13
14											14
15											15

11-1 RECYCLING PROBLEM (continued)

1., 6.   **ACCOUNTS RECEIVABLE LEDGER**

CUSTOMER Joan Aberg   CUSTOMER NO. 110

DATE		ITEM	POST. REF.	DEBIT	CREDIT	DEBIT BALANCE
20-- Aug.	1	Balance	✔			2 4 9 90

CUSTOMER Joe Chapin   CUSTOMER NO. 120

DATE		ITEM	POST. REF.	DEBIT	CREDIT	DEBIT BALANCE

CUSTOMER Susan King   CUSTOMER NO. 130

DATE		ITEM	POST. REF.	DEBIT	CREDIT	DEBIT BALANCE

CUSTOMER Gary Voyles   CUSTOMER NO. 140

DATE		ITEM	POST. REF.	DEBIT	CREDIT	DEBIT BALANCE
20-- Aug.	1	Balance	✔			3 6 7 50

1., 6.   **ACCOUNTS PAYABLE LEDGER**

VENDOR **Boot Town**   VENDOR NO. 210

DATE		ITEM	POST. REF.	DEBIT	CREDIT	CREDIT BALANCE
Aug.	1	Balance	✔			2 0 7 2 00

VENDOR **Diamond T. Boots**   VENDOR NO. 220

DATE		ITEM	POST. REF.	DEBIT	CREDIT	CREDIT BALANCE

VENDOR **National Supply**   VENDOR NO. 230

DATE		ITEM	POST. REF.	DEBIT	CREDIT	CREDIT BALANCE

VENDOR **Western Leather Co.**   VENDOR NO. 240

DATE		ITEM	POST. REF.	DEBIT	CREDIT	CREDIT BALANCE
Aug.	1	Balance	✔			3 2 7 6 00

VENDOR **Yeatman Corporation**   VENDOR NO. 250

DATE		ITEM	POST. REF.	DEBIT	CREDIT	CREDIT BALANCE
Aug.	1	Balance	✔			3 5 0 0 00

11-1   RECYCLING PROBLEM (continued)

6.

1., 2., 3., 4., 5., 6.   **GENERAL LEDGER**

ACCOUNT Cash   ACCOUNT NO. 1110

DATE		ITEM	POST. REF.	DEBIT	CREDIT	BALANCE	
						DEBIT	CREDIT
20-- Aug.	1	Balance	✔			15 840 00	

ACCOUNT Accounts Receivable   ACCOUNT NO. 1130

DATE		ITEM	POST. REF.	DEBIT	CREDIT	BALANCE	
						DEBIT	CREDIT
20-- Aug.	1	Balance	✔			6 17 40	

ACCOUNT Supplies—Office   ACCOUNT NO. 1145

DATE		ITEM	POST. REF.	DEBIT	CREDIT	BALANCE	
						DEBIT	CREDIT
20-- Aug.	1	Balance	✔			2 196 00	

ACCOUNT Supplies—Store   ACCOUNT NO. 1150

DATE		ITEM	POST. REF.	DEBIT	CREDIT	BALANCE	
						DEBIT	CREDIT
20-- Aug.	1	Balance	✔			1 872 00	

ACCOUNT Accounts Payable   ACCOUNT NO. 2110

DATE		ITEM	POST. REF.	DEBIT	CREDIT	BALANCE	
						DEBIT	CREDIT
20-- Aug.	1	Balance	✔				8 848 00

11-1 RECYCLING PROBLEM (continued)

ACCOUNT Sales Tax Payable ACCOUNT NO. 2120

DATE		ITEM	POST. REF.	DEBIT	CREDIT	BALANCE DEBIT	BALANCE CREDIT
20-- Aug.	1	Balance	✔				1 1 2 5 00

ACCOUNT Sales ACCOUNT NO. 4110

DATE		ITEM	POST. REF.	DEBIT	CREDIT	BALANCE DEBIT	BALANCE CREDIT
20-- Aug.	1	Balance	✔				180 0 0 0 00

ACCOUNT Sales Returns and Allowances ACCOUNT NO. 4130

DATE		ITEM	POST. REF.	DEBIT	CREDIT	BALANCE DEBIT	BALANCE CREDIT
20-- Aug.	1	Balance	✔			1 5 1 8 11	

ACCOUNT Purchases ACCOUNT NO. 5110

DATE		ITEM	POST. REF.	DEBIT	CREDIT	BALANCE DEBIT	BALANCE CREDIT
20-- Aug.	1	Balance	✔			105 6 0 0 00	

ACCOUNT Purchases Discount ACCOUNT NO. 5120

DATE		ITEM	POST. REF.	DEBIT	CREDIT	BALANCE DEBIT	BALANCE CREDIT
20-- Aug.	1	Balance	✔				2 1 1 0 50

ACCOUNT Purchases Returns and Allowances — ACCOUNT NO. 5130

DATE		ITEM	POST. REF.	DEBIT	CREDIT	BALANCE DEBIT	BALANCE CREDIT
20-- Aug.	1	Balance	✔				1 5 4 8 00

ACCOUNT Advertising Expense — ACCOUNT NO. 6105

DATE		ITEM	POST. REF.	DEBIT	CREDIT	BALANCE DEBIT	BALANCE CREDIT
20-- Aug.	1	Balance	✔			2 7 7 0 00	

ACCOUNT Cash Short and Over — ACCOUNT NO. 6110

DATE		ITEM	POST. REF.	DEBIT	CREDIT	BALANCE DEBIT	BALANCE CREDIT
20-- Aug.	1	Balance	✔			1 4 11	

ACCOUNT Miscellaneous Expense — ACCOUNT NO. 6135

DATE		ITEM	POST. REF.	DEBIT	CREDIT	BALANCE DEBIT	BALANCE CREDIT
20-- Aug.	1	Balance	✔			1 5 2 0 00	

ACCOUNT Rent Expense — ACCOUNT NO. 6145

DATE		ITEM	POST. REF.	DEBIT	CREDIT	BALANCE DEBIT	BALANCE CREDIT
20-- Aug.	1	Balance	✔			9 1 0 0 00	

ACCOUNT Utilities Expense — ACCOUNT NO. 6170

DATE		ITEM	POST. REF.	DEBIT	CREDIT	BALANCE DEBIT	BALANCE CREDIT
20-- Aug.	1	Balance	✔			2 2 6 0 00	

Preparing a semimonthly payroll

1.

PAYROLL REGISTER

SEMIMONTHLY PERIOD ENDED July 31, 20 – –   DATE OF PAYMENT July 31, 20 – –

	EMPL. NO.	EMPLOYEE'S NAME	MARI-TAL STATUS	NO. OF ALLOW-ANCES	EARNINGS			DEDUCTIONS						NET PAY	CHECK NO.	
					REGULAR	OVERTIME	TOTAL	FEDERAL INCOME TAX	SOC. SEC. TAX	MEDICARE TAX	HEALTH INSURANCE	OTHER	TOTAL			
					1	2	3	4	5	6	7	8	9	10		
1	5	Abrams, Thomas	S	1	892 00						35 00					1
2	6	Carroll, John	M	2	880 00	90 00					60 00					2
3	1	Harris, Jonathan	S	1	924 00						35 00					3
4	4	Kennard, Mary	S	1	1056 00	72 00					35 00					4
5	2	Locke, Anna	M	2	994 00						60 00					5
6	7	Rayford, Stan	M	2	812 00						60 00					6
7	3	Suell, Nicole	M	3	860 00						80 00					7
8																8
9																9
10																10
11																11
12																12

2., 3.

Check stub (NO. 621):

NO. **621**

Date: _____ 20___ $________________

To: ________________

____

For: ________________

BAL. BRO'T. FOR'D		
AMT. DEPOSITED		
TOTAL		
AMT. THIS CHECK		
BAL. CAR'D. FOR'D		

Check (NO. 621):

GENERAL ACCOUNT   NO. **621**   66-877 / 530

SANFORD COMPANY

________________ 20 _______

PAY TO THE ORDER OF ________________________________ $ __________

____ DOLLARS

For Classroom Use Only

Peoples Bank and Trust

Charlotte, NC 28206-8444

⑈053008774⑈ 196⑈2236⑈42⑈

Check stub (CHECK NO. 558):

CHECK NO. **558**

PERIOD ENDING		
EARNINGS	$	
REG.	$	
O.T.	$	
DEDUCTIONS	$	
INC. TAX	$	
SOC. SEC. TAX	$	
MED. TAX	$	
HEALTH INS.	$	
OTHER	$	
NET PAY	$	

Check (NO. 558):

PAYROLL ACCOUNT   66-877 / 530

________________ 20 _______   NO. **558**

PAY TO THE ORDER OF ________________________________ $ __________

____ DOLLARS

For Classroom Use Only

SANFORD COMPANY

Peoples Bank and Trust

Charlotte, NC 28206-8444

⑈053008774⑈ 982⑈561⑈4732

Check stub (CHECK NO. 562):

CHECK NO. **562**

PERIOD ENDING		
EARNINGS	$	
REG.	$	
O.T.	$	
DEDUCTIONS	$	
INC. TAX	$	
SOC. SEC. TAX	$	
MED. TAX	$	
HEALTH INS.	$	
OTHER	$	
NET PAY	$	

Check (NO. 562):

PAYROLL ACCOUNT   66-877 / 530

________________ 20 _______   NO. **562**

PAY TO THE ORDER OF ________________________________ $ __________

____ DOLLARS

For Classroom Use Only

SANFORD COMPANY

Peoples Bank and Trust

Charlotte, NC 28206-8444

⑈053008774⑈ 982⑈561⑈4732

13-1 RECYCLING PROBLEM, p. E-10

Journalizing payroll transactions

1.

GENERAL JOURNAL   PAGE 10

	DATE		ACCOUNT TITLE	DOC. NO.	POST. REF.	DEBIT	CREDIT	
1								1
2								2
3								3
4								4
5								5
6								6
7								7
8								8
9								9
10								10
11								11
12								12
13								13
14								14
15								15
16								16
17								17
18								18
19								19
20								20
21								21
22								22
23								23
24								24
25								25

RECYCLING PROBLEM (concluded)

1., 2.

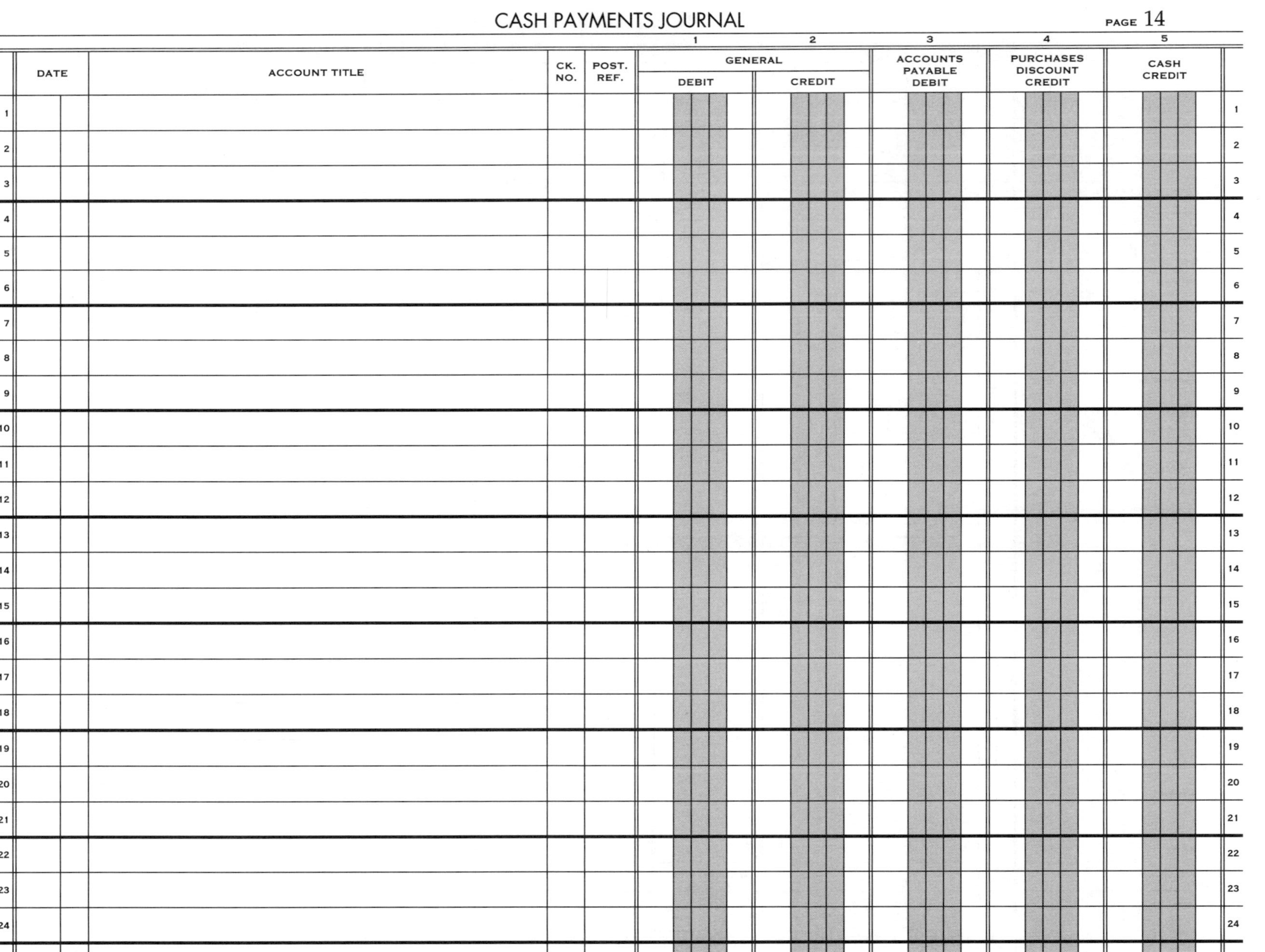

CASH PAYMENTS JOURNAL   PAGE 14

	DATE	ACCOUNT TITLE	CK. NO.	POST. REF.	GENERAL		ACCOUNTS PAYABLE DEBIT	PURCHASES DISCOUNT CREDIT	CASH CREDIT	
					1 DEBIT	2 CREDIT	3	4	5	
1										1
2										2
3										3
4										4
5										5
6										6
7										7
8										8
9										9
10										10
11										11
12										12
13										13
14										14
15										15
16										16
17										17
18										18
19										19
20										20
21										21
22										22
23										23
24										24

14-1 RECYCLING PROBLEM, p. E-11

Preparing an 8-column work sheet for a merchandising business

1., 2.

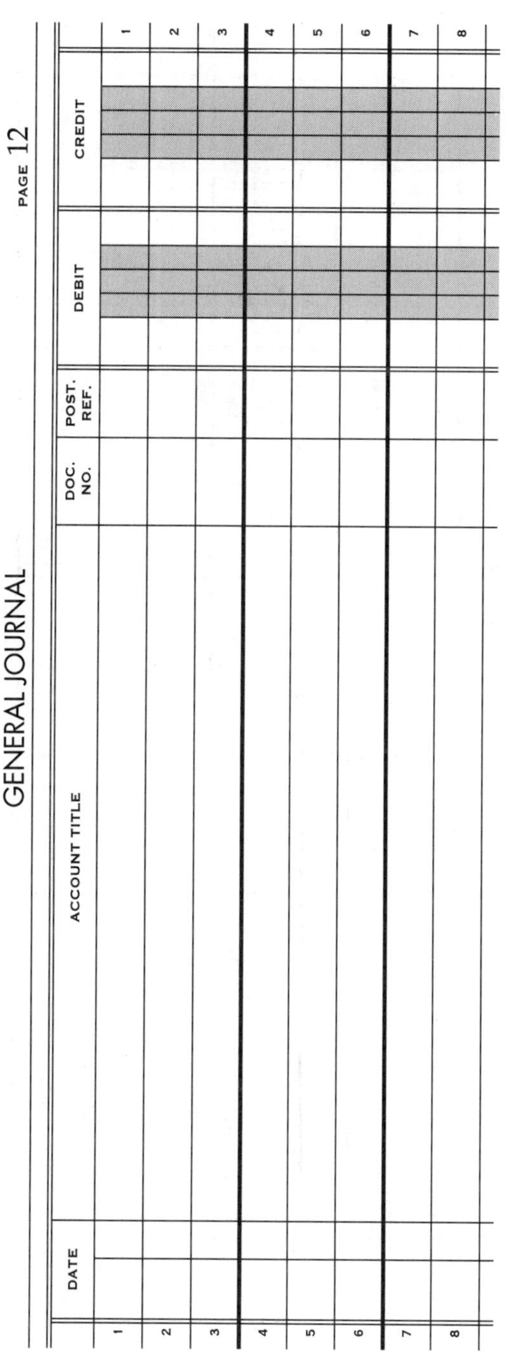

1., 5.

Audio Source, Inc.

Work Sheet

For Year Ended December 31, 20 – –

	Account Title	Trial Balance Debit	Trial Balance Credit	Adjustments Debit	Adjustments Credit	Income Statement Debit	Income Statement Credit	Balance Sheet Debit	Balance Sheet Credit
1	Cash	24 640 00							
2	Petty Cash	500 00							
3	Accounts Receivable	24 480 82							
4	Allow. for Uncoll. Accts.		148 33						
5	Merchandise Inventory	267 980 00							
6	Supplies—Office	6 100 00							
7	Supplies—Store	6 500 00							
8	Prepaid Insurance	5 160 00							
9	Office Equipment	37 483 00							
10	Acc. Depr.—Office Equipment		22 489 00						
11	Store Equipment	25 489 00							
12	Acc. Depr.—Store Equipment		16 493 00						
13	Accounts Payable		11 665 00						
14	Federal Income Tax Payable								
15	Emp. Income Tax Payable		650 00						
16	Social Security Tax Payable		757 76						
17	Medicare Tax Payable		177 22						
18	Sales Tax Payable		1 140 00						
19	Unemployment Tax Pay.—Fed.		41 60						
20	Unemployment Tax Pay.—State		280 80						
21	Health Ins. Premiums Pay.		140 00						
22	U.S. Savings Bonds Payable		60 00						
23	United Way Donations Pay.		45 00						
24	Dividends Payable		7 500 00						
25	Capital Stock		100 000 00						
26	Retained Earnings		99 977 67						

Before Federal Income Tax

Total of Income Statement Credit column __________

Total of Income Statement Debit column __________

Net Income before Federal Income Tax __________

14-1 RECYCLING PROBLEM (concluded)

Audio Source, Inc.

Work Sheet

For Year Ended December 31, 20 – –

#	ACCOUNT TITLE	Trial Balance Debit (1)	Trial Balance Credit (2)	Adjustments Debit (3)	Adjustments Credit (4)	Income Statement Debit (5)	Income Statement Credit (6)	Balance Sheet Debit (7)	Balance Sheet Credit (8)
27	Dividends	30 000 00							
28	Income Summary								
29	Sales		887 450 00						
30	Sales Discount	5 118 36							
31	Sales Returns and Allowances	7 184 69							
32	Purchases	402 300 00							
33	Purchases Discount		4 118 18						
34	Purch. Returns and Allowances		10 140 48						
35	Advertising Expense	5 680 00							
36	Cash Short and Over	12 15							
37	Credit Card Fee Expense	2 315 00							
38	Depr. Exp.—Office Equipment								
39	Depr. Exp.—Store Equipment								
40	Insurance Expense								
41	Miscellaneous Expense	2 830 00							
42	Payroll Taxes Expense	27 851 58							
43	Rent Expense	17 280 00							
44	Salary Expense	201 094 44							
45	Supplies Expense—Office								
46	Supplies Expense—Store								
47	Uncollectible Accts. Expense								
48	Utilities Expense	3 275 00							
49	Federal Income Tax Expense	6 000 00							
50									
51									
52									

Federal Income Tax	Rate	Tax
First $50,000	____	________
Next $25,000	____	________
Next $25,000	____	________
________ − $100,000.00 = ________	____	________
Total Federal Income Tax		________

15-1 RECYCLING PROBLEM, p. E-11

Preparing financial statements

Hawkins Parts, Inc.

Work Sheet

For Year Ended December 31, 20 – –

	ACCOUNT TITLE	TRIAL BALANCE DEBIT	TRIAL BALANCE CREDIT	ADJUSTMENTS DEBIT	ADJUSTMENTS CREDIT	INCOME STATEMENT DEBIT	INCOME STATEMENT CREDIT	BALANCE SHEET DEBIT	BALANCE SHEET CREDIT	
1	Cash	14158 00						14158 00		1
2	Petty Cash	250 00						250 00		2
3	Accounts Receivable	22184 22						22184 22		3
4	Allow. for Uncoll. Accts.		148 33		(e) 2656 00				2804 33	4
5	Merchandise Inventory	231148 25		(d) 4819 00				235967 25		5
6	Supplies—Office	8125 00			(a) 6950 00			1175 00		6
7	Supplies—Store	4819 36			(b) 4418 11			401 25		7
8	Prepaid Insurance	12800 00			(c) 12000 00			800 00		8
9	Office Equipment	33148 00						33148 00		9
10	Acc. Depr.—Office Equipment		18440 00		(f) 5148 00				23588 00	10
11	Store Equipment	42184 00						42184 00		11
12	Acc. Depr.—Store Equipment		22994 00		(g) 4184 00				27178 00	12
13	Accounts Payable		22154 00						22154 00	13
14	Federal Income Tax Payable				(h) 12807 72				12807 72	14
15	Emp. Income Tax Payable		720 00						720 00	15
16	Social Security Tax Payable		647 78						647 78	16
17	Medicare Tax Payable		151 50						151 50	17
18	Sales Tax Payable		4154 00						4154 00	18
19	Unemployment Tax Pay.—Fed.		64 00						64 00	19
20	Unemployment Tax Pay.—State		432 00						432 00	20
21	Health Ins. Premiums Pay.		200 00						200 00	21
22	U.S. Savings Bonds Payable		80 00						80 00	22
23	United Way Donations Pay.		60 00						60 00	23
24	Dividends Payable		10000 00						10000 00	24
25	Capital Stock		320000 00						320000 00	25
26	Retained Earnings		1120039 95						1120039 95	26

Hawkins Parts, Inc.

Work Sheet

For Year Ended December 31, 20 – –

	ACCOUNT TITLE	TRIAL BALANCE		ADJUSTMENTS		INCOME STATEMENT		BALANCE SHEET		
		1 DEBIT	2 CREDIT	3 DEBIT	4 CREDIT	5 DEBIT	6 CREDIT	7 DEBIT	8 CREDIT	
27	Dividends	40 000 00						40 000 00		27
28	Income Summary				(d) 4 819 00		4 819 00			28
29	Sales		928 148 06				928 148 06			29
30	Sales Discount	4 148 08				4 148 08				30
31	Sales Returns and Allowances	6 114 99				6 114 99				31
32	Purchases	414 810 09				414 810 09				32
33	Purchases Discount		3 184 07				3 184 07			33
34	Purch. Returns and Allowances		9 448 97				9 448 97			34
35	Advertising Expense	25 110 05				25 110 05				35
36	Cash Short and Over	25 05				25 05				36
37	Credit Card Fee Expense	6 480 02				6 480 02				37
38	Depr. Exp.—Office Equipment			(f) 5 148 00		5 148 00				38
39	Depr. Exp.—Store Equipment			(g) 4 184 00		4 184 00				39
40	Insurance Expense			(c) 12 000 00		12 000 00				40
41	Miscellaneous Expense	16 481 00				16 481 00				41
42	Payroll Taxes Expense	23 481 55				23 481 55				42
43	Rent Expense	16 000 00				16 000 00				43
44	Salary Expense	189 480 91				189 480 91				44
45	Supplies Expense—Office			(a) 6 950 00		6 950 00				45
46	Supplies Expense—Store			(b) 4 418 11		4 418 11				46
47	Uncollectible Accts. Expense			(e) 2 656 00		2 656 00				47
48	Utilities Expense	4 118 09				4 118 09				48
49	Federal Income Tax Expense	50 000 00		(h) 12 807 72		62 807 72				49
50		1165 066 66	1165 066 66	52 982 83	52 982 83	804 413 66	945 600 10	390 267 72	249 081 28	50
51	Net Inc. after Federal Inc. Tax					141 186 44			141 186 44	51
52						945 600 10	945 600 10	390 267 72	390 267 72	52

15-1 RECYCLING PROBLEM (continued)

1.

										% OF NET SALES

2.

15-1 RECYCLING PROBLEM (continued)

3.

4.

Earnings per Share

Net Income after Federal Income Tax	÷	Number of Shares Outstanding	=	Earnings per Share
$	÷		=	$

Price-Earnings Ratio

Market Price per Share	÷	Earnings per Share	=	Price-Earnings Ratio
$	÷	$	=	

16-1 RECYCLING PROBLEM, p. E-12

Journalizing and posting adjusting and closing entries; preparing a post-closing trial balance

1.

GENERAL JOURNAL

PAGE 18

	DATE	ACCOUNT TITLE	DOC. NO.	POST. REF.	DEBIT	CREDIT	
1							1
2							2
3							3
4							4
5							5
6							6
7							7
8							8
9							9
10							10
11							11
12							12
13							13
14							14
15							15
16							16
17							17
18							18
19							19
20							20
21							21
22							22
23							23
24							24
25							25
26							26
27							27
28							28
29							29
30							30
31							31
32							32

3.

GENERAL JOURNAL   PAGE 19

	DATE	ACCOUNT TITLE	DOC. NO.	POST. REF.	DEBIT	CREDIT	
1							1
2							2
3							3
4							4
5							5
6							6
7							7
8							8
9							9
10							10
11							11
12							12
13							13
14							14
15							15
16							16
17							17
18							18
19							19
20							20
21							21
22							22
23							23
24							24
25							25
26							26
27							27
28							28
29							29
30							30
31							31
32							32
33							33

16-1 RECYCLING PROBLEM (continued)

2., 4., 5.   **GENERAL LEDGER**

ACCOUNT **Cash**   ACCOUNT NO. 1110

DATE		ITEM	POST. REF.	DEBIT	CREDIT	BALANCE DEBIT	BALANCE CREDIT
20-- Dec.	31	Balance	✔			11 3 2 6 40	

ACCOUNT **Petty Cash**   ACCOUNT NO. 1120

DATE		ITEM	POST. REF.	DEBIT	CREDIT	BALANCE DEBIT	BALANCE CREDIT
20-- Dec.	31	Balance	✔			2 0 0 00	

ACCOUNT **Accounts Receivable**   ACCOUNT NO. 1130

DATE		ITEM	POST. REF.	DEBIT	CREDIT	BALANCE DEBIT	BALANCE CREDIT
20-- Dec.	31	Balance	✔			17 7 4 7 38	

ACCOUNT **Allow. for Uncoll. Accts.**   ACCOUNT NO. 1135

DATE		ITEM	POST. REF.	DEBIT	CREDIT	BALANCE DEBIT	BALANCE CREDIT
20-- Dec.	31	Balance	✔				1 1 8 66

ACCOUNT **Merchandise Inventory**   ACCOUNT NO. 1140

DATE		ITEM	POST. REF.	DEBIT	CREDIT	BALANCE DEBIT	BALANCE CREDIT
20-- Dec.	31	Balance	✔			184 9 1 8 60	

ACCOUNT **Supplies—Office**   ACCOUNT NO. 1145

DATE		ITEM	POST. REF.	DEBIT	CREDIT	BALANCE DEBIT	BALANCE CREDIT
20-- Dec.	31	Balance	✔			6 5 0 0 00	

GENERAL LEDGER

ACCOUNT Supplies—Store   ACCOUNT NO. 1150

DATE		ITEM	POST. REF.	DEBIT	CREDIT	BALANCE	
						DEBIT	CREDIT
20-- Dec.	31	Balance	✔			3 8 5 5 49	

ACCOUNT Prepaid Insurance   ACCOUNT NO. 1160

DATE		ITEM	POST. REF.	DEBIT	CREDIT	BALANCE	
						DEBIT	CREDIT
20-- Dec.	31	Balance	✔			10 2 4 0 00	

ACCOUNT Office Equipment   ACCOUNT NO. 1205

DATE		ITEM	POST. REF.	DEBIT	CREDIT	BALANCE	
						DEBIT	CREDIT
20-- Dec.	31	Balance	✔			26 5 1 8 40	

ACCOUNT Acc. Depr.—Office Equipment   ACCOUNT NO. 1210

DATE		ITEM	POST. REF.	DEBIT	CREDIT	BALANCE	
						DEBIT	CREDIT
20-- Dec.	31	Balance	✔				14 7 5 2 00

ACCOUNT Store Equipment   ACCOUNT NO. 1215

DATE		ITEM	POST. REF.	DEBIT	CREDIT	BALANCE	
						DEBIT	CREDIT
20-- Dec.	31	Balance	✔			33 7 4 7 20	

ACCOUNT Acc. Depr.—Store Equipment   ACCOUNT NO. 1220

DATE		ITEM	POST. REF.	DEBIT	CREDIT	BALANCE	
						DEBIT	CREDIT
20-- Dec.	31	Balance	✔				18 3 9 5 20

16-1   RECYCLING PROBLEM (continued)

GENERAL LEDGER

ACCOUNT Accounts Payable   ACCOUNT NO. 2110

DATE	ITEM	POST. REF.	DEBIT	CREDIT	BALANCE DEBIT	BALANCE CREDIT
20-- Dec. 31	Balance	✔				17 7 2 3 20

ACCOUNT Federal Income Tax Payable   ACCOUNT NO. 2120

DATE	ITEM	POST. REF.	DEBIT	CREDIT	BALANCE DEBIT	BALANCE CREDIT

ACCOUNT Employee Income Tax Payable   ACCOUNT NO. 2130

DATE	ITEM	POST. REF.	DEBIT	CREDIT	BALANCE DEBIT	BALANCE CREDIT
20-- Dec. 31	Balance	✔				5 7 6 00

ACCOUNT Social Security Tax Payable   ACCOUNT NO. 2135

DATE	ITEM	POST. REF.	DEBIT	CREDIT	BALANCE DEBIT	BALANCE CREDIT
20-- Dec. 31	Balance	✔				5 1 8 22

ACCOUNT Medicare Tax Payable   ACCOUNT NO. 2140

DATE	ITEM	POST. REF.	DEBIT	CREDIT	BALANCE DEBIT	BALANCE CREDIT
20-- Dec. 31	Balance	✔				1 2 1 20

ACCOUNT Sales Tax Payable   ACCOUNT NO. 2145

DATE	ITEM	POST. REF.	DEBIT	CREDIT	BALANCE DEBIT	BALANCE CREDIT
20-- Dec. 31	Balance	✔				3 3 2 3 20

ACCOUNT Unemployment Tax Payable—Federal   ACCOUNT NO. 2150

DATE	ITEM	POST. REF.	DEBIT	CREDIT	BALANCE DEBIT	BALANCE CREDIT
20-- Dec. 31	Balance	✔				5 1 20

GENERAL LEDGER

ACCOUNT Unemployment Tax Payable—State
ACCOUNT NO. 2155

DATE	ITEM	POST. REF.	DEBIT	CREDIT	BALANCE DEBIT	BALANCE CREDIT
Dec. 31	Balance	✔			3 4 5 60	

ACCOUNT Health Insurance Premiums Payable
ACCOUNT NO. 2160

DATE	ITEM	POST. REF.	DEBIT	CREDIT	BALANCE DEBIT	BALANCE CREDIT
Dec. 31	Balance	✔				1 6 0 00

ACCOUNT U.S. Savings Bonds Payable
ACCOUNT NO. 2165

DATE	ITEM	POST. REF.	DEBIT	CREDIT	BALANCE DEBIT	BALANCE CREDIT
Dec. 31	Balance	✔			6 4 00	

ACCOUNT United Way Donations Payable
ACCOUNT NO. 2170

DATE	ITEM	POST. REF.	DEBIT	CREDIT	BALANCE DEBIT	BALANCE CREDIT
Dec. 31	Balance	✔				4 8 00

ACCOUNT Dividends Payable
ACCOUNT NO. 2180

DATE	ITEM	POST. REF.	DEBIT	CREDIT	BALANCE DEBIT	BALANCE CREDIT
Dec. 31	Balance	✔				8 0 0 00

ACCOUNT Capital Stock
ACCOUNT NO. 3110

DATE	ITEM	POST. REF.	DEBIT	CREDIT	BALANCE DEBIT	BALANCE CREDIT
Dec. 31	Balance	✔				25 6 0 0 00

16-1 RECYCLING PROBLEM (continued)

GENERAL LEDGER

ACCOUNT **Retained Earnings** ACCOUNT NO. 3120

DATE	ITEM	POST. REF.	DEBIT	CREDIT	BALANCE DEBIT	BALANCE CREDIT
20-- Dec. 1	Balance	✔				89 6 3 1 96

ACCOUNT **Dividends** ACCOUNT NO. 3130

DATE	ITEM	POST. REF.	DEBIT	CREDIT	BALANCE DEBIT	BALANCE CREDIT
20-- Dec. 31	Balance	✔			32 0 0 0 00	

ACCOUNT **Income Summary** ACCOUNT NO. 3140

DATE	ITEM	POST. REF.	DEBIT	CREDIT	BALANCE DEBIT	BALANCE CREDIT

ACCOUNT **Sales** ACCOUNT NO. 4110

DATE	ITEM	POST. REF.	DEBIT	CREDIT	BALANCE DEBIT	BALANCE CREDIT
20-- Dec. 31	Balance	✔				742 5 1 8 45

ACCOUNT **Sales Discount** ACCOUNT NO. 4120

DATE	ITEM	POST. REF.	DEBIT	CREDIT	BALANCE DEBIT	BALANCE CREDIT
20-- Dec. 31	Balance	✔			3 3 1 8 46	

ACCOUNT **Sales Returns and Allowances** ACCOUNT NO. 4130

DATE	ITEM	POST. REF.	DEBIT	CREDIT	BALANCE DEBIT	BALANCE CREDIT
20-- Dec. 31	Balance	✔			4 8 9 1 99	

GENERAL LEDGER

ACCOUNT Purchases   ACCOUNT NO. 5110

DATE	ITEM	POST. REF.	DEBIT	CREDIT	BALANCE DEBIT	BALANCE CREDIT
20-- Dec. 31	Balance	✔			331 848 07	

ACCOUNT Purchases Discount   ACCOUNT NO. 5120

DATE	ITEM	POST. REF.	DEBIT	CREDIT	BALANCE DEBIT	BALANCE CREDIT
20-- Dec. 31	Balance	✔				2 547 26

ACCOUNT Purch. Returns and Allowances   ACCOUNT NO. 5130

DATE	ITEM	POST. REF.	DEBIT	CREDIT	BALANCE DEBIT	BALANCE CREDIT
20-- Dec. 31	Balance	✔				7 559 18

ACCOUNT Advertising Expense   ACCOUNT NO. 6105

DATE	ITEM	POST. REF.	DEBIT	CREDIT	BALANCE DEBIT	BALANCE CREDIT
20-- Dec. 31	Balance	✔			20 088 04	

ACCOUNT Cash Short and Over   ACCOUNT NO. 6107

DATE	ITEM	POST. REF.	DEBIT	CREDIT	BALANCE DEBIT	BALANCE CREDIT
20-- Dec. 31	Balance	✔			20 04	

ACCOUNT Credit Card Fee Expense   ACCOUNT NO. 6110

DATE	ITEM	POST. REF.	DEBIT	CREDIT	BALANCE DEBIT	BALANCE CREDIT
20-- Dec. 31	Balance	✔			5 184 02	

16-1   RECYCLING PROBLEM (continued)

GENERAL LEDGER

ACCOUNT Depr. Exp.—Office Equipment   ACCOUNT NO. 6115

DATE	ITEM	POST. REF.	DEBIT	CREDIT	BALANCE DEBIT	BALANCE CREDIT

ACCOUNT Depr. Exp.—Store Equipment   ACCOUNT NO. 6120

DATE	ITEM	POST. REF.	DEBIT	CREDIT	BALANCE DEBIT	BALANCE CREDIT

ACCOUNT Insurance Expense   ACCOUNT NO. 6125

DATE	ITEM	POST. REF.	DEBIT	CREDIT	BALANCE DEBIT	BALANCE CREDIT

ACCOUNT Miscellaneous Expense   ACCOUNT NO. 6130

DATE	ITEM	POST. REF.	DEBIT	CREDIT	BALANCE DEBIT	BALANCE CREDIT
20-- Dec. 31	Balance	✔			13 1 8 4 80	

ACCOUNT Payroll Taxes Expense   ACCOUNT NO. 6135

DATE	ITEM	POST. REF.	DEBIT	CREDIT	BALANCE DEBIT	BALANCE CREDIT
20-- Dec. 31	Balance	✔			18 7 8 5 24	

ACCOUNT Rent Expense   ACCOUNT NO. 6140

DATE	ITEM	POST. REF.	DEBIT	CREDIT	BALANCE DEBIT	BALANCE CREDIT
20-- Dec. 31	Balance	✔			12 8 0 0 00	

  RECYCLING PROBLEM (continued)

GENERAL LEDGER

ACCOUNT **Salary Expense** ACCOUNT NO. 6145

DATE	ITEM	POST. REF.	DEBIT	CREDIT	BALANCE DEBIT	BALANCE CREDIT
20-- Dec. 31	Balance	✔			151 584 73	

ACCOUNT **Supplies Expense—Office** ACCOUNT NO. 6150

DATE	ITEM	POST. REF.	DEBIT	CREDIT	BALANCE DEBIT	BALANCE CREDIT

ACCOUNT **Supplies Expense—Store** ACCOUNT NO. 6155

DATE	ITEM	POST. REF.	DEBIT	CREDIT	BALANCE DEBIT	BALANCE CREDIT

ACCOUNT **Uncollectible Accounts Expense** ACCOUNT NO. 6160

DATE	ITEM	POST. REF.	DEBIT	CREDIT	BALANCE DEBIT	BALANCE CREDIT

ACCOUNT **Utilities Expense** ACCOUNT NO. 6170

DATE	ITEM	POST. REF.	DEBIT	CREDIT	BALANCE DEBIT	BALANCE CREDIT
20-- Dec. 31	Balance	✔			3 294 47	

ACCOUNT **Federal Income Tax Expense** ACCOUNT NO. 7105

DATE	ITEM	POST. REF.	DEBIT	CREDIT	BALANCE DEBIT	BALANCE CREDIT
20-- Dec. 31	Balance	✔			40 000 00	

16-1 RECYCLING PROBLEM (concluded)

5.

ACCOUNT TITLE	DEBIT	CREDIT

17-1 RECYCLING PROBLEM, p. E-13

Recording entries for uncollectible accounts

1.

GENERAL JOURNAL

PAGE 10

	DATE	ACCOUNT TITLE	DOC. NO.	POST. REF.	DEBIT	CREDIT	
1							1
2							2
3							3
4							4

2.

GENERAL JOURNAL

PAGE 11

	DATE	ACCOUNT TITLE	DOC. NO.	POST. REF.	DEBIT	CREDIT	
1							1
2							2
3							3
4							4
5							5
6							6

3.

GENERAL JOURNAL

PAGE 12

	DATE	ACCOUNT TITLE	DOC. NO.	POST. REF.	DEBIT	CREDIT	
1							1
2							2
3							3
4							4
5							5
6							6

4.

GENERAL JOURNAL

PAGE 13

	DATE	ACCOUNT TITLE	DOC. NO.	POST. REF.	DEBIT	CREDIT	
1							1
2							2
3							3

2.

CASH RECEIPTS JOURNAL

PAGE 11

					1	2	3	4	5	6	7	
				GENERAL			ACCOUNTS RECEIVABLE CREDIT	SALES CREDIT	SALES TAX PAYABLE CREDIT	SALES DISCOUNT DEBIT	CASH DEBIT	
	DATE	ACCOUNT TITLE	DOC. NO.	POST. REF.	DEBIT	CREDIT						
1												1
2												2
3												3
4												4
5												5
6												6
7												7
8												8
9												9
10												10

3.

CASH RECEIPTS JOURNAL

PAGE 12

					1	2	3	4	5	6	7	
				GENERAL			ACCOUNTS RECEIVABLE CREDIT	SALES CREDIT	SALES TAX PAYABLE CREDIT	SALES DISCOUNT DEBIT	CASH DEBIT	
	DATE	ACCOUNT TITLE	DOC. NO.	POST. REF.	DEBIT	CREDIT						
1												1
2												2
3												3
4												4
5												5
6												6
7												7
8												8
9												9

17-1   RECYCLING PROBLEM (continued)

1., 2., 3., 4.   **GENERAL LEDGER**

ACCOUNT Cash   ACCOUNT NO. 1105

DATE		ITEM	POST. REF.	DEBIT	CREDIT	BALANCE DEBIT	BALANCE CREDIT
Oct.	1	Balance	✔			4 9 7 8 00	

ACCOUNT Accounts Receivable   ACCOUNT NO. 1125

DATE		ITEM	POST. REF.	DEBIT	CREDIT	BALANCE DEBIT	BALANCE CREDIT
Oct.	1	Balance	✔			62 4 8 6 25	

ACCOUNT Allowance for Uncollectible Accounts   ACCOUNT NO. 1130

DATE		ITEM	POST. REF.	DEBIT	CREDIT	BALANCE DEBIT	BALANCE CREDIT
Oct.	1	Balance	✔				2 4 1 8 19

ACCOUNT Uncollectible Accounts Expense   ACCOUNT NO. 6165

DATE		ITEM	POST. REF.	DEBIT	CREDIT	BALANCE DEBIT	BALANCE CREDIT

1., 2., 3.   **ACCOUNTS RECEIVABLE LEDGER**

CUSTOMER Agnew Company   CUSTOMER NO. 110

DATE		ITEM	POST. REF.	DEBIT	CREDIT	DEBIT BALANCE
June	7		S6	8 0 4 24		8 0 4 24

CUSTOMER Chittenden Corp.   CUSTOMER NO. 120

DATE		ITEM	POST. REF.	DEBIT	CREDIT	DEBIT BALANCE
May	13		S5	2 8 4 75		2 8 4 75

CUSTOMER Dionne, Inc.   CUSTOMER NO. 130

DATE		ITEM	POST. REF.	DEBIT	CREDIT	DEBIT BALANCE
Jan.	1	Balance	✔			4 6 8 30
Mar.	3	Written off	G3		4 6 8 30	—

CUSTOMER Foster Corp.   CUSTOMER NO. 140

DATE		ITEM	POST. REF.	DEBIT	CREDIT	DEBIT BALANCE
June	21		S6	5 7 4 10		5 7 4 10

CUSTOMER Grant Company   CUSTOMER NO. 150

DATE		ITEM	POST. REF.	DEBIT	CREDIT	DEBIT BALANCE
Jan.	1	Balance	✔			7 0 5 18

Name ___________________________ Date ___________ Class ___________

Recording transactions for plant assets

1.

CASH PAYMENTS JOURNAL

PAGE 1

		CK. NO.	POST. REF.	GENERAL DEBIT	GENERAL CREDIT	ACCOUNTS PAYABLE DEBIT	PURCHASES DISCOUNT CREDIT	CASH CREDIT
DATE	ACCOUNT TITLE			1	2	3	4	5

5.

CASH RECEIPTS JOURNAL

PAGE 2

		DOC. NO.	POST. REF.	GENERAL DEBIT	GENERAL CREDIT	ACCOUNTS RECEIVABLE CREDIT	SALES CREDIT	SALES TAX PAYABLE CREDIT	SALES DISCOUNT DEBIT	CASH DEBIT
DATE	ACCOUNT TITLE			1	2	3	4	5	6	7

2., 4., 6.

PLANT ASSET RECORD No. ____ General Ledger Account No. _______

Description _______________________ General Ledger Account ________________

Date Bought _______________ Serial Number __________ Original Cost _______________

Estimated Useful Life _____________ Estimated Salvage Value __________ Depreciation Method _______________

Disposed of: Discarded __________ Sold _________ Traded _________________
Date ____________________ Disposal Amount _____________________

YEAR	ANNUAL DEPRECIATION EXPENSE	ACCUMULATED DEPRECIATION	ENDING BOOK VALUE

Continue record on back of card

3.

Plant asset: ___________________ Original cost: __________
Depreciation method: _________________ Estimated salvage value: __________
Estimated useful life: __________

Year	Beginning Book Value	Declining-Balance Rate	Annual Depreciation	Ending Book Value

18-1   RECYCLING PROBLEM (continued)

2., 4., 6.

PLANT ASSET RECORD No. _____   General Ledger Account No. _______

Description _________________________   General Ledger Account _______________

Date Bought _________________   Serial Number ___________   Original Cost _______________

Estimated Useful Life _____________   Estimated Salvage Value ___________   Depreciation Method _______________

Disposed of: Discarded __________   Sold _________   Traded _______________

Date _________________________   Disposal Amount _______________

YEAR	ANNUAL DEPRECIATION EXPENSE	ACCUMULATED DEPRECIATION	ENDING BOOK VALUE

Continue record on back of card

3.

Plant asset: _____________________   Original cost: __________

Depreciation method: _________________   Estimated salvage value: __________

Estimated useful life: __________

Year	Beginning Book Value	Annual Depreciation	Accumulated Depreciation	Ending Book Value

5.

GENERAL JOURNAL

PAGE 2

	DATE	ACCOUNT TITLE	DOC. NO.	POST. REF.	DEBIT	CREDIT	
1							1
2							2
3							3
4							4
5							5
6							6
7							7
8							8
9							9
10							10
11							11
12							12
13							13
14							14
15							15
16							16
17							17
18							18
19							19
20							20
21							21
22							22
23							23
24							24
25							25
26							26
27							27
28							28
29							29
30							30
31							31
32							32
33							33

19-1 RECYCLING PROBLEM, p. E-14

Determining the cost of inventory using the fifo, lifo, and weighted-average inventory costing methods

1.

FIFO Method

Purchase Dates	Units Purchased	Unit Price	Total Cost	FIFO Units on Hand	FIFO Cost
January 1, beginning inventory					
January 3, purchases					
March 29, purchases					
August 15, purchases					
November 13, purchases					
Totals					

LIFO Method

Purchase Dates	Units Purchased	Unit Price	Total Cost	LIFO Units on Hand	LIFO Cost
January 1, beginning inventory					
January 3, purchases					
March 29, purchases					
August 15, purchases					
November 13, purchases					
Totals					

Weighted-Average Method

Purchases			Total Cost
Date	Units	Unit Price	
January 1, beginning inventory			
January 3, purchases			
March 29, purchases			
August 15, purchases			
November 13, purchases			
Totals			

	Fifo	Lifo	Weighted Average

2.

Highest Cost of Merchandise Sold:

20-1 RECYCLING PROBLEM, p. E-14

Journalizing notes payable and notes receivable transactions

1.

GENERAL JOURNAL   PAGE 3

DATE	ACCOUNT TITLE	DOC. NO.	POST. REF.	DEBIT	CREDIT

1.

CASH RECEIPTS JOURNAL   PAGE 6

DATE	ACCOUNT TITLE	DOC. NO.	POST. REF.	GENERAL DEBIT	GENERAL CREDIT	ACCOUNTS RECEIVABLE CREDIT	SALES CREDIT	SALES TAX PAYABLE CREDIT	SALES DISCOUNT DEBIT	CASH DEBIT

2.

20-1 RECYCLING PROBLEM (concluded)

3.

CASH PAYMENTS JOURNAL

PAGE 10

DATE	ACCOUNT TITLE	CK. NO.	POST. REF.	GENERAL DEBIT	GENERAL CREDIT	ACCOUNTS PAYABLE DEBIT	PURCHASES DISCOUNT CREDIT	CASH CREDIT
				1	2	3	4	5

21-1 RECYCLING PROBLEM, p. E-15

Journalizing and posting entries for accrued interest revenue and expense

1.

Farrell Company

Work Sheet

For Year Ended December 31, 20X1

	ACCOUNT TITLE	TRIAL BALANCE		ADJUSTMENTS	
		DEBIT	CREDIT	DEBIT	CREDIT
4	Interest Receivable				
15	Interest Payable				
50	Interest Income		1 8 9 7 00		
51	Interest Expense	2 4 5 8 00			

2., 3.

GENERAL JOURNAL　　　　　　　　　　　　　PAGE 15

	DATE	ACCOUNT TITLE	DOC. NO.	POST. REF.	DEBIT	CREDIT	
1							1
2							2
3							3
4							4
5							5
6							6
7							7
8							8
9							9
10							10
11							11

4.

GENERAL JOURNAL　　　　　　　　　　　　　PAGE 16

	DATE	ACCOUNT TITLE	DOC. NO.	POST. REF.	DEBIT	CREDIT	
1							1
2							2
3							3
4							4
5							5

2., 3., 4., 5., 6. **GENERAL LEDGER**

ACCOUNT Notes Receivable   ACCOUNT NO. 1115

DATE	ITEM	POST. REF.	DEBIT	CREDIT	BALANCE DEBIT	BALANCE CREDIT
Nov. 9		G14	800 00		800 00	

ACCOUNT Interest Receivable   ACCOUNT NO. 1120

DATE	ITEM	POST. REF.	DEBIT	CREDIT	BALANCE DEBIT	BALANCE CREDIT

ACCOUNT Notes Payable   ACCOUNT NO. 2105

DATE	ITEM	POST. REF.	DEBIT	CREDIT	BALANCE DEBIT	BALANCE CREDIT
Dec. 14		CR12		4 800 00		4 800 00

ACCOUNT Interest Payable   ACCOUNT NO. 2110

DATE	ITEM	POST. REF.	DEBIT	CREDIT	BALANCE DEBIT	BALANCE CREDIT

21-1   RECYCLING PROBLEM (continued)

2., 3., 4., 5., 6.   **GENERAL LEDGER**

ACCOUNT **Income Summary**   ACCOUNT NO. **3120**

DATE		ITEM	POST. REF.	DEBIT	CREDIT	BALANCE DEBIT	BALANCE CREDIT

ACCOUNT **Interest Income**   ACCOUNT NO. **7110**

DATE		ITEM	POST. REF.	DEBIT	CREDIT	BALANCE DEBIT	BALANCE CREDIT
Dec.	31		CR12		8 5 00		1 8 9 7 00

ACCOUNT **Interest Expense**   ACCOUNT NO. **8105**

DATE		ITEM	POST. REF.	DEBIT	CREDIT	BALANCE DEBIT	BALANCE CREDIT
Dec.	31		CP12	1 0 0 00		2 4 8 5 00	

5.

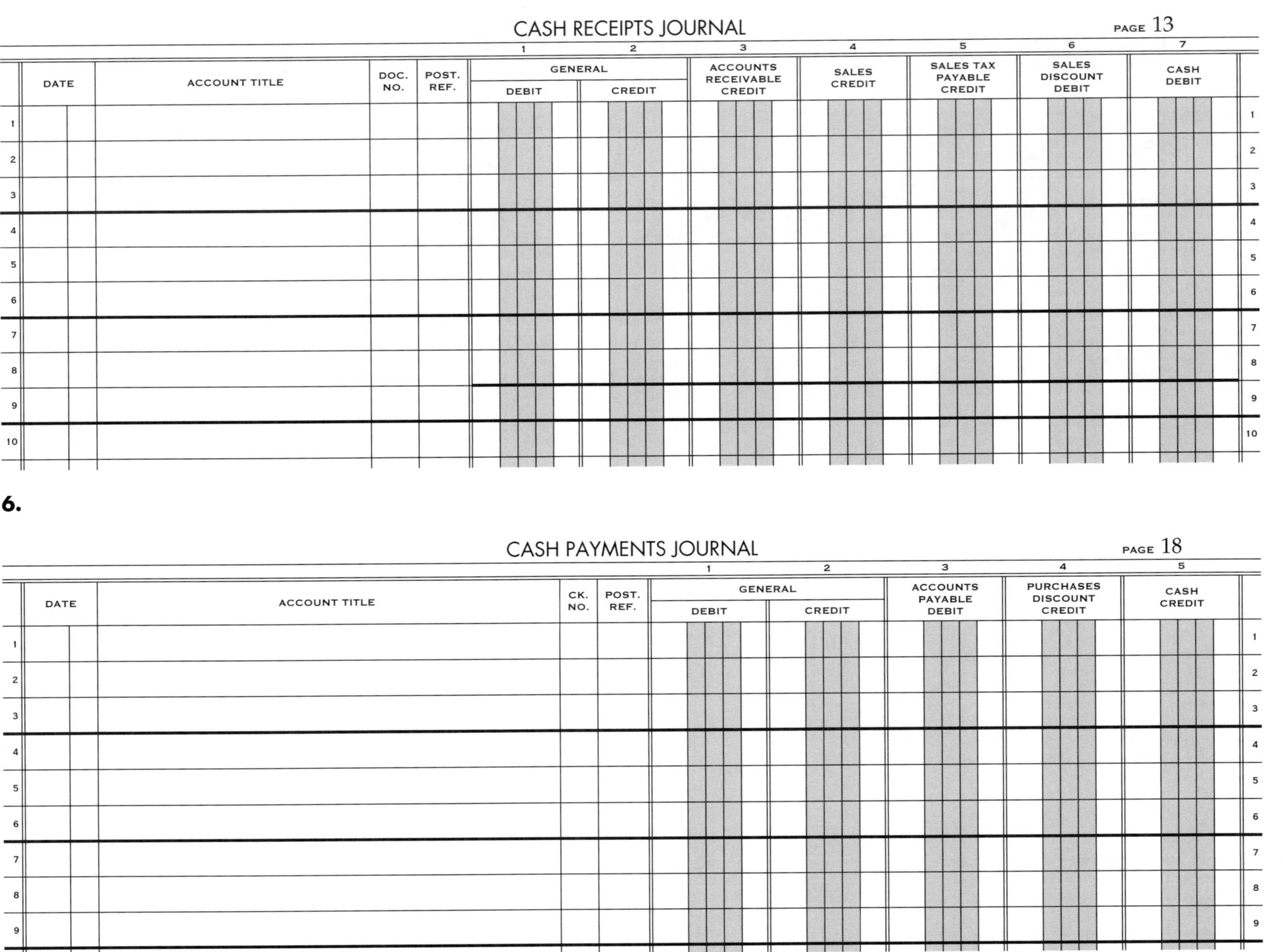

CASH RECEIPTS JOURNAL PAGE 13

	DATE	ACCOUNT TITLE	DOC. NO.	POST. REF.	GENERAL		ACCOUNTS RECEIVABLE CREDIT	SALES CREDIT	SALES TAX PAYABLE CREDIT	SALES DISCOUNT DEBIT	CASH DEBIT	
					DEBIT	CREDIT						
					1	2	3	4	5	6	7	
1												1
2												2
3												3
4												4
5												5
6												6
7												7
8												8
9												9
10												10

6.

CASH PAYMENTS JOURNAL PAGE 18

	DATE	ACCOUNT TITLE	CK. NO.	POST. REF.	GENERAL		ACCOUNTS PAYABLE DEBIT	PURCHASES DISCOUNT CREDIT	CASH CREDIT	
					DEBIT	CREDIT				
					1	2	3	4	5	
1										1
2										2
3										3
4										4
5										5
6										6
7										7
8										8
9										9

[This page left blank intentionally]

RECYCLING PROBLEM, p. E-16

Preparing financial statements and end-of-fiscal-period entries for a corporation

1.

Applewhite Corporation

Work Sheet

For Year Ended December 31, 20 – –

	ACCOUNT TITLE	TRIAL BALANCE DEBIT (1)	TRIAL BALANCE CREDIT (2)	ADJUSTMENTS DEBIT (3)	ADJUSTMENTS CREDIT (4)	INCOME STATEMENT DEBIT (5)	INCOME STATEMENT CREDIT (6)	BALANCE SHEET DEBIT (7)	BALANCE SHEET CREDIT (8)
1	Cash	2 0 1 4 00							
2	Petty Cash	4 0 0 00							
3	Notes Receivable	3 2 0 0 00							
4	Interest Receivable								
5	Accounts Receivable	100 6 7 8 00							
6	Allowance for Uncoll. Accts.		2 2 8 00						
7	Merchandise Inventory	230 6 5 4 46							
8	Supplies	5 1 8 5 02							
9	Prepaid Insurance	11 2 0 0 00							
10	Office Equipment	23 3 1 8 58							
11	Accum. Depr.—Office Equip.		6 9 6 8 00						
12	Store Equipment	21 7 2 7 00							
13	Accum. Depr.—Store Equip.		14 5 2 8 00						
14	Notes Payable		2 0 0 0 0 00						
15	Interest Payable								
16	Accounts Payable		2 5 7 2 6 62						
17	Employee Income Tax Payable		1 9 6 7 04						
18	Federal Income Tax Payable								
19	Social Security Tax Payable		1 6 9 7 05						
20	Medicare Tax Payable		4 1 0 15						
21	Sales Tax Payable		2 0 1 4 93						
22	Unemploy. Tax Pay.—Fed.		3 6 48						
23	Unemploy. Tax Pay.—State		2 3 4 24						
24	Health Ins. Premiums Pay.		5 3 7 00						
25	Dividends Payable		6 4 0 0 00						
26	Capital Stock		120 0 0 0 00						
27	Retained Earnings		118 9 9 0 40						
28	Dividends	2 5 6 0 0 00							

Before Federal Income Tax

Total of Income Statement Credit column   ____________

Total of Income Statement Debit column   ____________

Net Income before Federal Income Tax   ____________

22-1 RECYCLING PROBLEM (continued)

Applewhite Corporation

Work Sheet

For Year Ended December 31, 20 – –

	ACCOUNT TITLE	TRIAL BALANCE DEBIT	TRIAL BALANCE CREDIT	ADJUSTMENTS DEBIT	ADJUSTMENTS CREDIT	INCOME STATEMENT DEBIT	INCOME STATEMENT CREDIT	BALANCE SHEET DEBIT	BALANCE SHEET CREDIT	
29	Income Summary									29
30	Sales		1801 5 1 4 54							30
31	Sales Discount	4 7 1 5 49								31
32	Sales Returns and Allowances	12 3 8 9 91								32
33	Purchases	1198 5 4 6 46								33
34	Purchases Discount		10 4 9 4 42							34
35	Purchases Ret. and Allow.		4 9 4 7 33							35
36	Advertising Expense	13 1 8 9 52								36
37	Cash Short and Over	1 3 50								37
38	Credit Card Fee Expense	6 7 9 1 46								38
39	Depr. Exp.—Office Equip.									39
40	Depr. Exp.—Store Equip.									40
41	Insurance Expense									41
42	Miscellaneous Expense	33 7 4 9 04								42
43	Payroll Taxes Expense	25 7 4 7 22								43
44	Rent Expense	36 0 0 0 00								44
45	Repair Expense	4 9 2 3 99								45
46	Salary Expense	337 2 3 8 69								46
47	Supplies Expense									47
48	Uncollectible Accounts Exp.									48
49	Utilities Expense	16 3 5 6 50								49
50	Gain on Plant Assets		1 2 3 8 40							50
51	Interest Income		5 1 8 40							51
52	Interest Expense	2 8 8 0 00								52
53	Loss on Plant Assets	1 9 3 2 16								53
54	Federal Income Tax Expense	20 0 0 0 00								54
55		2138 4 5 1 00	2138 4 5 1 00							55
56	Net Inc. after Fed. Inc. Tax									56
57										57

Federal Income Tax   Rate   Tax

First $50,000   ____   ________

Next $25,000   ____   ________

__________ – $75,000.00 = __________   ____   ________

Total Federal Income Tax   ________

 RECYCLING PROBLEM (continued)

2.

Applewhite Corporation

Income Statement

For Year Ended December 31, 20 – –

					% OF NET SALES

22-1 RECYCLING PROBLEM (continued)

Applewhite Corporation

Income Statement (continued)

For Year Ended December 31, 20 – –

		% OF NET SALES

4.

Applewhite Corporation

Statement of Stockholders' Equity

For Year Ended December 31, 20 – –

RECYCLING PROBLEM (continued)

5.

Applewhite Corporation

Balance Sheet

December 31, 20 – –

22-1 RECYCLING PROBLEM (continued)

3.

Income Statement Analysis

	Acceptable %	Actual %	Positive Result		Recommended Action If Needed
			Yes	**No**	
Cost of merchandise sold	Not more than 68.0%				
Gross profit on operations	Not less than 32.0%				
Total operating expenses	Not more than 25.0%				
Income from operations	Not less than 7.0%				
Net deduction from other revenue and expenses	Not more than 0.5%				
Net income before federal income tax	Not less than 6.5%				

6.

Balance Sheet Analysis

	Acceptable	Actual	Positive Result		Recommended Action If Needed
			Yes	**No**	
Working capital	Not less than $250,000.00				
Current ratio	Between 4.0 to 1 and 6.0 to 1				

17.

GENERAL JOURNAL   PAGE 15

	DATE		ACCOUNT TITLE	DOC. NO.	POST. REF.	DEBIT	CREDIT	
1								1
2								2
3								3
4								4
5								5
6								6
7								7
8								8
9								9
10								10
11								11
12								12
13								13
14								14
15								15
16								16
17								17
18								18
19								19
20								20
21								21

22-1 RECYCLING PROBLEM (continued)

18.

GENERAL JOURNAL

PAGE 16

	DATE	ACCOUNT TITLE	DOC. NO.	POST. REF.	DEBIT	CREDIT	
1							1
2							2
3							3
4							4
5							5
6							6
7							7
8							8
9							9
10							10
11							11
12							12
13							13
14							14
15							15
16							16
17							17
18							18
19							19
20							20
21							21
22							22
23							23
24							24
25							25
26							26
27							27
28							28
29							29
30							30
31							31
32							32
33							33

 RECYCLING PROBLEM (concluded)

19.

GENERAL JOURNAL

PAGE 17

	DATE	ACCOUNT TITLE	DOC. NO.	POST. REF.	DEBIT	CREDIT	
1							1
2							2
3							3
4							4
5							5
6							6
7							7
8							8
9							9
10							10

Name ______________________ Date ______________ Class ______________

23-1 RECYCLING PROBLEM, p. E-17

Recording partners' investments and withdrawals, preparing financial statements, and liquidating a partnership

1., 5.

CASH RECEIPTS JOURNAL

PAGE 11

	DATE	ACCOUNT TITLE	DOC. NO.	POST. REF.	1 GENERAL DEBIT	2 GENERAL CREDIT	3 ACCOUNTS RECEIVABLE CREDIT	4 SALES CREDIT	5 SALES DISCOUNT DEBIT	6 CASH DEBIT	
1											1
2											2
3											3
4											4
5											5
6											6
7											7
8											8
9											9
10											10
11											11
12											12
13											13
14											14
15											15
16											16
17											17
18											18
19											19
20											20
21											21
22											22
23											23
24											24
25											25

2., 5.

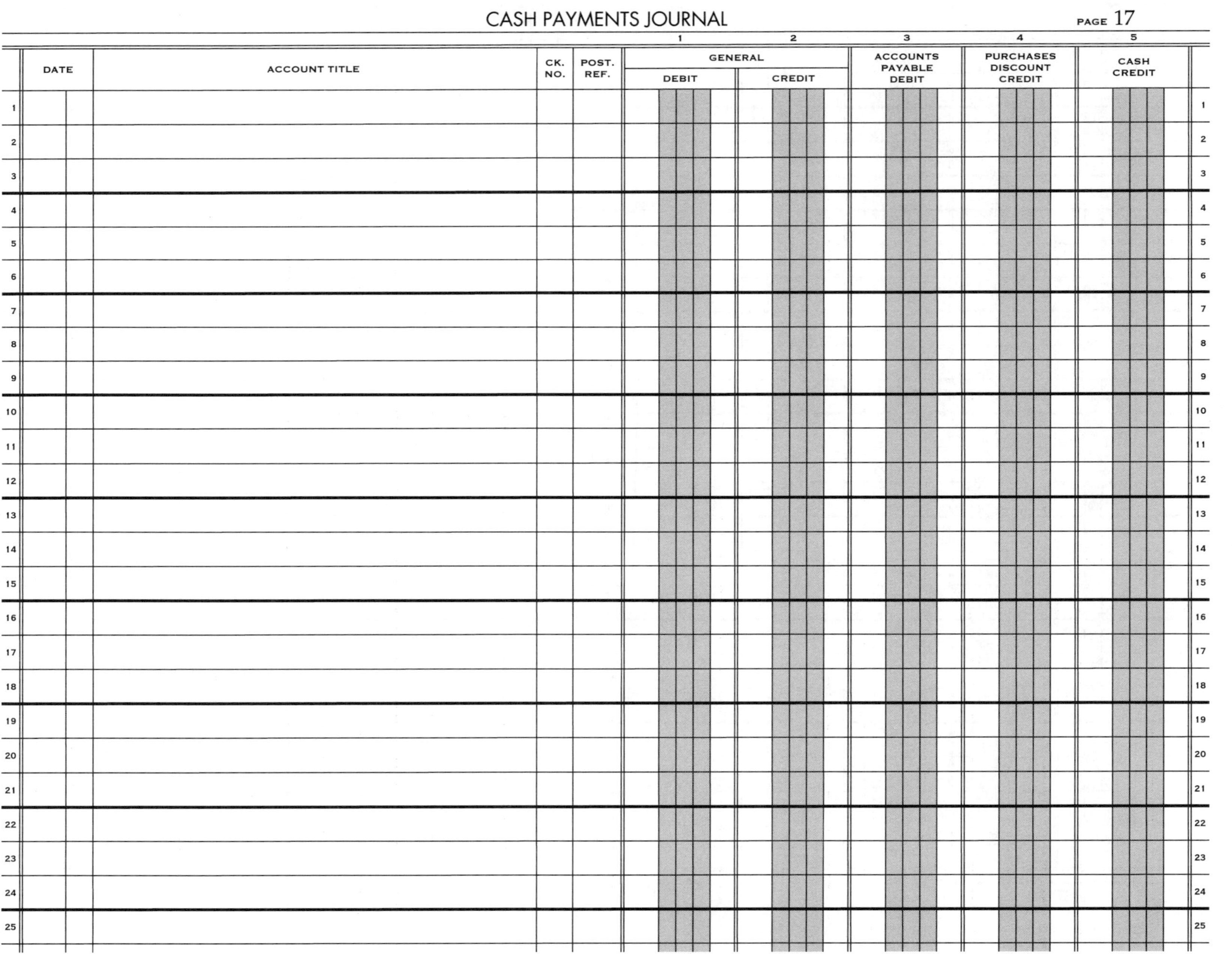

CASH PAYMENTS JOURNAL — PAGE 17

DATE	ACCOUNT TITLE	CK. NO.	POST. REF.	GENERAL		ACCOUNTS PAYABLE DEBIT	PURCHASES DISCOUNT CREDIT	CASH CREDIT	
				DEBIT (1)	CREDIT (2)	(3)	(4)	(5)	
1									1
2									2
3									3
4									4
5									5
6									6
7									7
8									8
9									9
10									10
11									11
12									12
13									13
14									14
15									15
16									16
17									17
18									18
19									19
20									20
21									21
22									22
23									23
24									24
25									25

23-1 RECYCLING PROBLEM (continued)

2., 5.

GENERAL JOURNAL   PAGE 21

	DATE		ACCOUNT TITLE	DOC. NO.	POST. REF.	DEBIT	CREDIT	
1								1
2								2
3								3
4								4
5								5
6								6
7								7
8								8
9								9
10								10
11								11
12								12
13								13
14								14
15								15
16								16
17								17
18								18
19								19
20								20
21								21
22								22
23								23
24								24
25								25
26								26
27								27
28								28
29								29
30								30
31								31
32								32
33								33

3.

23-1 RECYCLING PROBLEM (concluded)

4.

24-1 RECYCLING PROBLEM, p. E-18

Recording international and Internet sales

1., 2.

CASH RECEIPTS JOURNAL

PAGE 23

		DATE	ACCOUNT TITLE	DOC. NO.	POST. REF.	GENERAL DEBIT	GENERAL CREDIT	ACCOUNTS RECEIVABLE CREDIT	SALES CREDIT	SALES DISCOUNT DEBIT	CASH DEBIT	
						1	2	3	4	5	6	
1												1
2												2
3												3
4												4
5												5
6												6
7												7
8												8
9												9
10												10
11												11
12												12
13												13
14												14
15												15
16												16
17												17
18												18
19												19
20												20
21												21
22												22
23												23
24												24
25												25

  RECYCLING PROBLEM (concluded)

1.

GENERAL JOURNAL   PAGE 23

	DATE	ACCOUNT TITLE	DOC. NO.	POST. REF.	DEBIT	CREDIT	
1							1
2							2
3							3
4							4
5							5
6							6
7							7
8							8
9							9
10							10
11							11
12							12
13							13
14							14
15							15
16							16
17							17
18							18
19							19
20							20
21							21
22							22
23							23
24							24
25							25
26							26
27							27
28							28
29							29
30							30
31							31
32							32
33							33

Extra form

Extra form

Extra form

% OF SALES

Extra form

Extra form

JOURNAL

	DATE	ACCOUNT TITLE	DOC. NO.	POST. REF.	GENERAL 1 DEBIT	GENERAL 2 CREDIT	SALES CREDIT 3	CASH 4 DEBIT	CASH 5 CREDIT	
1										1
2										2
3										3
4										4
5										5
6										6
7										7
8										8
9										9
10										10
11										11
12										12
13										13
14										14
15										15
16										16
17										17
18										18
19										19
20										20
21										21
22										22
23										23
24										24
25										25

Extra form

JOURNAL

| PAGE 5 | CASH CREDIT | CASH DEBIT | SALES CREDIT | GENERAL CREDIT | GENERAL DEBIT | POST. REF. | DOC. NO. | ACCOUNT TITLE | DATE |

Extra form

GENERAL JOURNAL

PAGE

	DATE		ACCOUNT TITLE	DOC. NO.	POST. REF.	DEBIT	CREDIT	
1								1
2								2
3								3
4								4
5								5
6								6
7								7
8								8
9								9
10								10
11								11
12								12
13								13
14								14
15								15
16								16
17								17
18								18
19								19
20								20
21								21
22								22
23								23
24								24
25								25
26								26
27								27
28								28
29								29
30								30
31								31
32								32
33								33

Extra form

GENERAL JOURNAL

PAGE

	DATE		ACCOUNT TITLE	DOC. NO.	POST. REF.	DEBIT	CREDIT	
1								1
2								2
3								3
4								4
5								5
6								6
7								7
8								8
9								9
10								10
11								11
12								12
13								13
14								14
15								15
16								16
17								17
18								18
19								19
20								20
21								21
22								22
23								23
24								24
25								25
26								26
27								27
28								28
29								29
30								30
31								31
32								32
33								33

GENERAL LEDGER

ACCOUNT   ACCOUNT NO.

DATE	ITEM	POST. REF.	DEBIT	CREDIT	BALANCE DEBIT	BALANCE CREDIT

ACCOUNT   ACCOUNT NO.

DATE	ITEM	POST. REF.	DEBIT	CREDIT	BALANCE DEBIT	BALANCE CREDIT

ACCOUNT   ACCOUNT NO.

DATE	ITEM	POST. REF.	DEBIT	CREDIT	BALANCE DEBIT	BALANCE CREDIT

ACCOUNT   ACCOUNT NO.

DATE	ITEM	POST. REF.	DEBIT	CREDIT	BALANCE DEBIT	BALANCE CREDIT

Extra forms

ACCOUNTS PAYABLE LEDGER

VENDOR ________________________________ VENDOR NO. ________

DATE	ITEM	POST. REF.	DEBIT	CREDIT	CREDIT BALANCE

VENDOR ________________________________ VENDOR NO. ________

DATE	ITEM	POST. REF.	DEBIT	CREDIT	CREDIT BALANCE

VENDOR ________________________________ VENDOR NO. ________

DATE	ITEM	POST. REF.	DEBIT	CREDIT	CREDIT BALANCE

VENDOR ________________________________ VENDOR NO. ________

DATE	ITEM	POST. REF.	DEBIT	CREDIT	CREDIT BALANCE

ACCOUNTS RECEIVABLE LEDGERS

CUSTOMER

CUSTOMER NO.

DATE	ITEM	POST. REF.	DEBIT	CREDIT	DEBIT BALANCE

CUSTOMER

CUSTOMER NO.

DATE	ITEM	POST. REF.	DEBIT	CREDIT	DEBIT BALANCE

CUSTOMER

CUSTOMER NO.

DATE	ITEM	POST. REF.	DEBIT	CREDIT	DEBIT BALANCE

CUSTOMER

CUSTOMER NO.

DATE	ITEM	POST. REF.	DEBIT	CREDIT	DEBIT BALANCE